Parenting Adhd

Practical Strategies for Parenting and Disciplining Your Child

(How to Be a Positive Parent to Grow Happy Child)

Lance Bartlett

Published by Rob Miles

© **Lance Bartlett**

All Rights Reserved

*Parenting **Adhd**: Practical Strategies for Parenting and Disciplining Your Child (How to Be a Positive Parent to Grow Happy Child)*

ISBN 978-1-990084-26-3

All rights reserved. No part of this guide may be reproduced in any form without permission in writing from the publisher except in the case of brief quotations embodied in critical articles or reviews.

Legal & Disclaimer

The information contained in this book is not designed to replace or take the place of any form of medicine or professional medical advice. The information in this book has been provided for educational and entertainment purposes only.

The information contained in this book has been compiled from sources deemed reliable, and it is accurate to the best of the Author's knowledge; however, the Author cannot guarantee its accuracy and validity and cannot be held liable for any errors or omissions. Changes are periodically made to this book. You must consult your doctor or get professional medical advice before using any of the suggested remedies, techniques, or information in this book.

Upon using the information contained in this book, you agree to hold harmless the Author from and against any damages, costs, and expenses, including any legal fees potentially resulting from the application of any of the information provided by this guide. This disclaimer applies to any damages or injury caused by the use and application, whether directly or indirectly, of any advice or information presented, whether for breach of contract, tort, negligence, personal injury, criminal intent, or under any other cause of action.

You agree to accept all risks of using the information presented inside this book.

You need to consult a professional medical practitioner in order to ensure you are both able and healthy enough to participate in this program.

Table of Contents

INTRODUCTION 1

CHAPTER 1: THE DILEMMA OF PARENTING 5

CHAPTER 2: PARENTING 101 – ON QUALITY TIME, HUMILITY, AND SELF RESPECT 9

CHAPTER 3: THE ESSENTIALS- CHARACTERISTICS OF A GOOD PARENT 19

CHAPTER 4: TEENAGERS REVEALED 39

CHAPTER 5: SPANKING AND YELLING ARE COUNTERPRODUCTIVE 47

CHAPTER 6: PARENTING SKILLS THAT WILL SHAPE YOUR CHILDREN 54

CHAPTER 7: IN A NUTSHELL 68

CHAPTER 8: RAISE YOUR TEENAGER PROPERLY THROUGH CONSCIOUS PARENTING 77

CHAPTER 9: COMMON PARENTING CHALLENGES IN THE TECH ERA 93

CHAPTER 10: ALWAYS TELL THE TRUTH 99

CHAPTER 11: HOLD A FAMILY MEETING EVERY WEEK ... 108

CHAPTER 12: HOW TO STOP SHOUTING AT THE CHILD? 112

CHAPTER 13: EXAMPLES OF GOOD PARENTING 117

CHAPTER 14: DEALING WITH TEMPER TANTRUMS 124

CHAPTER 15: MAKE TIME FOR YOUR CHILD 138

CHAPTER 16: FOCUS ON EDUCATION 144

CHAPTER 17: PARENTING STYLES 155

CHAPTER 18: COMMUNICATINGWITH TODDLERS 161

CHAPTER 19: ACCIDENTS HAPPEN 177

CONCLUSION 191

Introduction

Being a mother is probably the best job in the world. However, it is also one of the most difficult jobs in the world. The joy of bringing a newborn into this world or the bliss of holding a baby in your arms is incomparable.

With the changing social dynamics in the society, it is only natural to expect motherhood to progress and develop. In today's world, single moms are not only a common but also an encouraging phenomenon. This allows single women the autonomy to create their own families.

On the flipside, there is an overall lack of proper guidance on being a single mother, which is frustrating and disappointing.

Single parenting can be tricky, especially if you are not in it by choice.

If you have had a spouse or a partner who helped you with raising the kids, but circumstances force you to do the job on your own, then it can be frustrating and extremely demanding.

The desire to become a mother is instinctual in most women. There comes a time when women just know they are ready for motherhood. A woman may become a single mom by chance or by choice. However, there is no choice whatsoever when it comes to being a good mother.

Well, we doubt there is anything as a bad mother, as all mothers focus on the welfare of their child above anything else. But if you are unable to manage the responsibility, you may pose the question about your own capability to raise your kids. This scenario is not a cake walk, you will need help.

If you are a single mother, you know you have to manage it all singlehandedly. You have to play the role of a mother and a father. It may not be hunky dory and you may have to face a lot of difficulties. But it isn't impossible too. As long as you put your mind to it, there is absolutely nothing that can stop you from being an amazing parent (read mother).

The fact still remains that raising a child singlehandedly requires a lot of things to fall perfectly in place. This book will act as a guidebook to take on the role of a single parent. You can learn some practical tips that will help you traverse the path of being or becoming the best single mom.

Thanks again for downloading this book; I hope you find it helpful and informative.

Chapter 1: The Dilemma Of Parenting

For most parents, finding the balance between fatherhood and motherhood is actually one of the hardest things, next to moving a mountain. Depending on the age of your kids and the gender, several aspects come into play when it comes to the right kind of parenting approach. In most cases, the father is usually the disciplinarian, and the mother the more permissive parent, while in some cases, it normally works the other way around. Either way, the main thing to observe when talking about the all too hard subject of parenthood is to ensure that your kids grow up to be healthy adults in the long run. Healthy here has several meanings, including both physical and emotional well being. Before your son or daughter is set to leave your house, they should be conversant with essential interactive skills, probable eating habits, and divergent coping abilities in order to ensure a more well-rounded livelihood when on their own. If you fail this, not only will you come short of your parenting abilities, but your children will grow up into needy adults with at least one form of complication. One especially important detail to put into account is how your kids interact with each other. In fact, studies have shown that children, especially males, who do not interact well with their siblings when they are young have a higher likelihood of developing one form of depression later on in their lives. Of course, no one is perfect. There are certain instances that may prompt you into changing your parenting ways if it means protecting your child from potential hazardous influences, like substance abuse and so on. Have you ever wondered why certain successful

CEOs end up raising dead beat children? What do you think makes the difference? After all, they manage huge successful companies with countless employees under their command.

Children need both the parenting skills of a mother and father. In particular, they need the nurturing parenting style of a mother and the real world based and challenging parenting style of a father. However, the problem comes in the sense that, without an arrangement or cooperation, none of the styles can ever work separately. In fact, you will only end up frustrating each other. But before we get there, what exactly are the parenting styles used by most fathers, and what parenting styles are associated with most mothers? More importantly, how can you blend them together and make them work for the children as you prepare them for life? There is one caveat that stands out in this scenario. Sometimes these differing styles tend to vary with gender. Some families have the mother as the more demanding parent, and the father as the more nurturing parent. Regardless, when all is said and done, the point is to balance the different parenting styles and try to get the best from the blend. Let's take a look at some parenting styles that you can adopt when raising your kids.

Chapter 2: Parenting 101 – On Quality Time, Humility, And Self Respect

You are your child's world. They get up in the morning because you exist. The epicenter of their tiny world is you. They take comfort knowing that when they call out, you will immediately answer. Relatives, friends, or teachers will influence your child to varying degrees, but they do not have the ability to knead his/her character. It would definitely be you. Because you are your child's parent and he/she came into being because of you.

Today, majority of single parents are in paid work. And they do not have any choice for if they remain at home taking care of their children, bills cannot be paid. While the current trend may not have too much impact on a child-parent relationship, it could be alarming that it is only later in life that one can see how quickly time passes and when gone, it would be impossible to ask for re-run.

RULE #1 – Quality time is of the essence

Regardless if you are a working sole parent or not, sometimes, it is not really about the number of hours spent that makes all the difference but:

The quality of parent-child relationship

The sole parent's wellbeing and emotional stability

The attention given to the child especially when the custodial parent is around

The quality of care given to the child.

A working parent must ensure that he/she gives good attention to the child in the time that they are together. You may feel little enthusiasm especially after a hard day's of work, but you must make every effort that quality time spent with your child should be something he/she will remember as fun and worth it. Household chores and other errands must not be allowed to consume all your time together. To make all these possible, you need to eliminate activities that are usually on your routine. Ask yourself, are these activities more important than your time for your child? Once you have carved out the hours in your schedule, it would be easier for you to set your priorities. Remember the very purpose of quality time – instilling moral values to your child and teaching him/her the most important lessons of life. Among those are kindness, generosity, and thoughtfulness.

The following are some activities that you can do during quality time:

Eating out together

Going to a park

Riding a bike

Shopping

Attending church services

Playing computer or board games

Reading to your child before bedtime

Helping your child take a bath

Helping him/her prepare for school

Taking her swimming on a weekend

Teaching them to do household chores the fun way (you can have rewards after each chore is completed).

Making room for quality time does not necessarily mean totally eliminating activities, but rather modifying them. Instead of activities that separate you with your child, try arranging to do things as a family. Train your child the value of spending quality time with each other. If you take this matter seriously especially during the early growth years of your child, you will not get yourself into trouble later in life.

RULE #2 - Teach Your Child the Value of Humility

Many parents associate humility with weakness, and we do not want their children to be weak or easily manipulated. Parents want them strong, dependable, self-sufficient and independent. Humility is the starting point of all virtue. It means having the proper perspective and knowing that every person has equal worth. Teaching your child humility is important but would be challenging on your end. You cannot just demand this from him/her, but humility must be modeled. If you want your child to be respectful, you must respect others. If you want him/her to be successful, you must be as well. The same is true with humility. If you live it, your child will get it. Remember, they follow your lead and wait to see what you do. A parent's humility is a gift to his/her child.

What does humility have to do with kids being successful in life? The following are some of the answers:

Humility makes one feel significant – to fulfill your child's fullest potential, he must need to understand who he is and where he is heading to. This kind of understanding needs to be accurate. Humility is seeing oneself honestly. It will keep him grounded.

Humility prevents bullying and being bullied – When your child recognizes that all people are equal and never esteems himself above another, he will not consider asserting his superiority or take a bully's insult seriously.

Humility keeps one balanced - Humility will teach your child to become self-reliant and will make him realize that he is a part of a big community that must work hand in hand for the good of the whole. It will teach him to consider the needs of others and look outward rather than focusing on oneself.

RULE #3 – Teach Your Child Self-Respect

Respect starts in oneself. When your child is young, begin telling him that his body is special and needs to keep it that way. As he grows older, let him know that what he does in his body will have an impact in his overall well-being. For girls, as she come of age, let her know that the places an undergarment covers are very private and it is only Mom or her doctor are to see those private places. For boys, do not let them run around the house without their clothes on. Talk to him about clothes and what makes a man look more decent and presentable.

Teaching your child modesty will make him respect his body more. This is the kind of protection that you alone can give your child. This will give your child a sense of authority over his body, sexuality, and life. This way, when your child is ready to be all by himself/herself and explore the world, he/she will not give himself up that easy to someone who does not deserve his love.

Many parents make the mistake of trying not to interrupt and just stay in the background. They fear that being overprotective or controlling would only resort to losing their child in the process. Some single parents would give their child a token of their esteem (this could be an heirloom ring or a necklace) to remind them of their commitment to being responsible individuals. It is a reminder of what you expect and how highly you value them as your children.

Finally, let your child know your dreams about his future – good life, happiness, excellent health, and hopefully a successful marriage. Talk to your child in private and when you are both relaxed. Short walks are great or you can also do car trips. Doing this will make your child feel that he/she is important to you. And this influence can be lifelong.

Chapter 3: The Essentials- Characteristics Of A Good Parent

As a parent, there are days you will wonder if you really are a good parent. There are days you will feel like pulling out your hair in frustration. However, being a parent gets easier once you as the parent cultivates the right attitude and takes the right approach. This is especially effective if you prepare well before the arrival of your first child. Just like there are specific characteristics that must be within a successful entrepreneur, there are characteristics that every effective parent must cultivate within them before, during, and after childbirth. We shall begin our effective parenting manual by looking at the characteristics of a good parent.

Let us get started...

An active participant

In order to be an effective parent, you must cultivate participation. Participation means you must play an active role in your child's life. Here is a very important fact; children learn by observing their parents. If you project negativity, your children will project negativity. Why did I point that out? Because, if you approach parenting with negativity, chances are your child or children will catch on this (children are very intuitive).

You need to embrace your parenting role with a lot of zeal, compassion, enthusiasm and a clear but focused mind. Being an active participant in your child's life also means you take the time to learn and discover your child's personality. This will go a long way into helping you parent the child in accordance with their strengths, weaknesses, likes and dislikes.

Nurtures

Unconditional love is the backbone of every effective parent. Nurturing your child may mean demonstrating this love by focusing on the behavior of a child rather than the characteristic of the child when you want to apply any behavior correction. Nurturing is all about forgiving your child when he or she shows remorse for a wrong or misdeed. Additionally, nurturing is all about making allowances for age appropriate mistakes. It also means you have to employ positive reinforcement when setting limits for your child and keeping your perspective and expectation realistic as your child develops and grows.

A Good Teacher

So far, we have seen that children learn a lot by observing their parents. A large part of your job as a parent is to teach. You cannot be a good teacher if you do not love teaching. You would need to teach your child all the fundamental things he or she needs to develop into a holistic adult. You also have to remember that children are much easier to teach when they are younger, which means that you should model your child's behavior when he or she is younger. It means you should use this opportunity to impart common sense and wisdom in the child. As a teacher, you have to be alive to the fact that children respond better to lessons that are fun and creative. Therefore, you must make sure your lessons infuse a sense of new discovery and adventure.

An Effective Communicator

Effective communication is an integral part of the cohesiveness of a family. A parent needs to be the head of the family communication team. Communication means that the parent actively listens to the child and offers their opinion. Additionally, it means that the parent maintains eye contact during the conversation to make sure that the child understands what they have to say is important. Raising a child is not a dictatorship. To be an effective communicator, you also need to negotiate with your child on matters that matter to both of you and matters that concern his or her overall wellbeing and to make sure you are both on the same page.

Now that we have established the principles, or rather, the characters of a good parent, it is only right that we jump into the actual raising of the child. To start us off, we shall first look at some of the principles or strategies of parenting.

The Parenting Inner Circle - The Principles of Good Parenting

In the field of social science, parenting is the most researched area. While this may be the case, there is no specific manual or blueprint to being a good parent. However, throughout the entire study of the field of parenting, researchers all agree that there are some basic principles of parenting proven to contribute greatly to the process of raising a healthy and well-rounded child. With this in mind, it is also well to note that these principles are alive to the fact that at some instances, all a parent can do is react; react to situations that would otherwise not fall under the scope of these guiding principles. Additionally, you should note that following these principles does not automatically mean that parenting becomes a walk on the beach or that problems will not arise, no. These principles are no more scientific than the science behind being a good person. You should not take this to mean that the principles we shall look at are not effective, they are. In fact, researchers believe that raising your child using these principles will greatly reduce the chances of difficult behavior developing in the child.

What is good parenting? There are very many definitions of what good parenting is all about. In fact, it is true that each one of us has a view of what constitutes good parenting. With this in mind, let us try to put a definition to good parenting that we shall use while we discuss the guiding principles of parenting. In my view, I can define good parenting as parenting that nurtures psychological adjustments in behaviors such as honesty, kindness, self-reliance etc. Additionally, we can go further and define good parenting as parenting that helps children be all they can be in work, school etc; parenting that promotes development of the child's intellect and his or her desire to achieve.

We can go on and on and define good parenting in many ways, but I hope you get the picture of what constitutes good parenting. Now that we have exhausted that part of our introduction to the principles of parenting, let us look at the principles themselves. In total, there are ten known and proven principles. All the principles all have one aim and goal; to develop the child into a productive, responsible, and rounded adult. Let us look at these principles.

1st Principle: Your Actions Matter

One of the things that we have looked at, and seen so far is that children learn most of what they know by observation, so, your first principle is to be mindful of what you do and say in front of, and to your child. You have to be a mindful parent. This means your actions have to be intentional and not reactionary. Additionally, the more effort you put into being a mindful parent, the easier and instinctive it becomes. Being a mindful parent means you are a proactive parent rather than being a reactive parent. In addition, the difference between a child's character and the influence of his or her genes and the child and parent overall role in this development is astronomical. This means that what you do as a parent supersedes your child's genetic makeup. How so? Because your action as a parent is the basic guideline of how your child expresses the "genes," you often like to blame for any shortcomings your child may exhibit. Always remember; the greatest influence on your child and his or her development stems from you, the parent. You should always remind yourself this very critical fact; "what I do counts to my child's overall development."

As a parent, you should also aim to learn from your mistakes when you make them (which will be a lot, after all, parenting is not an exact art) rather than beating yourself up for mistakes. This matters because it influences the overall environment your child becomes exposed to over time. The truth is that if a parent is willing to admit their mistakes, the child will get the inclination to be more open about their shortcomings as well as being very respectful towards the parent. This is because it will cement the belief that the opinion of the child matters to the parent.

Do you also know that your actions play a major role in determining whether your children listen to you or not? If you are the kind of parent always telling their child to do this or the other and you somehow don't adhere to your own rules then it will be very difficult to get your child to do anything. If you have a rule that no one should have a phone or any technological gadget at the dinner table and somehow you think you are exempted because you are a parent, then you have got it all wrong. Act what you preach. Don't be the people who preach water but drink wine. Remember your child learns more from your actions rather than from what you say.

2nd Principle: There is Nothing like Being too Loving

I have heard many parents complain about how being too loving towards the child is a sure way to spoil them. Here is a shocker for you; spoiling a child with love does not exist. It is simply something "bad parents" conjured up as justification for their shortcomings. However, their reasoning is justified to some extent. Most parents view a show of love as giving the child "things" instead of love. When I talk of things, I do not necessarily mean material things. Things could be in the form of leniency, low expectations, as well as the very common material possessions. Genuine love (a love devoid of the above characteristics) helps your child develop a very strong sense of security, which makes them less needy. However, it is very important to distinguish between how you show affection to your child and how you do it. More often than not, children are very perceptive about genuine love and when you buy them off with one of the methods discussed above, they also know it.

What do we imply when we talk of genuine love? We are simply stating that you have to express physical affection. The moment your child is born (infant) and throughout childhood and all through adolescence, children need physical affection from the parent. Loving your child also means you praise any and every one of your child's accomplishments. Some parents worry that praising their children especially after positive achievement will make the child believe the parents love is conditional. This should not worry you if you express your affection and love at different time and not only when your child achieves a goal or is successful at something.

Remember however that loving your child unconditionally does not mean that you throw reason out the window. It is your responsibility to instill suitable morals into your child and not let them get away with everything because you think this is your way of showing love. Allowing your child to get away with everything will only lead to an adult who does not know what is wrong from right because they always got what they wanted and they always got away with everything. I am sure you would not want your child to turn out this way. Therefore, find a suitable balance between offering unconditional love and reason. This is critical since you don't want to be in a situation whereby when your child does something wrong and you punish them, they feel you don't love them at that particular moment. Your child should know that you care for them not because of what they do but rather because of who they are.

3rd Principle: Be Involved

A parent's involvement in the development of a child's mental health, happiness, and overall wellbeing is crucial. As the parent, you have to give your child a lot of special quality time, as much as you can spare. What you are doing with your child during the quality time is of no consequence. What is of consequence is how you do it. In most cases, the value of your quality time relies heavily on your state of mind and not on the activity at hand. In addition, being involved means that as the parent, you must show a keen interest in your child's interests. You should always remember that spending time doing what your child loves to do most is never a waste of time or energy. On a deeper level, children hold dear what is of value to the parent. Therefore, you should involve yourself in your child's school and schoolwork. If you involve yourself in your child's study from early childhood straight through college, your child will know that their education is something you hold dear and that their education is important to you.

4th Principle: Adapt

The fourth principle of good parenting is adapting your parenting style to meet your child development. "Good parenting is flexible". It is important to be alive to the fact that development of your child does not simply mean growing bigger in size; it means growing in terms of changes in your child's line of thought, feelings, capabilities, how they relate with others etc. It is possible to predict the stages of psychological development in your child. As a parent, you should make it a point to learn all you can about each developmental stage your child goes through long before they pass through these stages. This is so that you can prepare for the challenges. Additionally, your parenting style should be adoptive to the temperament of your child. You should not try to change or influence your child's disposition. Instead, you should aim to create situations and scenarios that exploit the advantages of your child's strengths. This also means that you should avoid situations that emphasize his or her weaknesses. The last bit of this parenting advice requires that you know what tickles your child and treating your child as a complete individual. While you should not change any of the fundamental principles of good parenting, being adaptive will require some tinkering with the principles to match your child's uniqueness. Adapting as a parent will also mean that you are very much aware of your changing role as a parent. At some point in your child's life, you will stop being the focal point in their life and become just one of the many people your child cares about; therefore, your parenting style should be adaptive to this fact and instead of controlling your child's life, a good parent should work to help the child control their own life.

5th Principle: Set Limits and Establish Rules

As a parent, you cannot overlook the importance of structure in your child's life. Over time, the limits and rules you set helps your child while he is developing his own behavior. Additionally, the structures you set for your child will provide some sort of security for your child's development. In addition, the structures imposed to design your child's behavior will at one point gradually cease to be external and become internal and part of the child's way of conceptualizing things. Your rules and limits should not titter on unfairness. You should be firm but also fair. One of the many jobs of a parent is to make sure that the child, despite their view on the world, does what is in their overall best interest. One of the major obstacles you are likely to encounter here is when your desire to be your child's friend clashes with your obligations as a parent. You should not construe this to mean that the rules you set for your child are just that, rules in writing, nor should it mean imposing your rules and limits just to show your child who is "the boss" or superior in the relationship. Your authority should be something your child deems to come from your many years of experience, good judgment, and wisdom, which all work to achieve the same goal i.e. foster cooperation. Additionally, you should always aim to know what your child is doing, with whom and where. More importantly, you should not take this to mean that you should spy on your child. While observing the activities of your child, you should do it in a way that does not demonstrate suspicion but demonstrates concern.

The second point to setting limits is that you should equip yourself with the prerequisite skill and knowledge for dealing with conflict over rules. Many parents are often times tempted to turn each dispute with their child into a battle that must have an outright winner and loser. So, how do you deal with such power struggles appropriately without making the child feel as though they have no control over their life and you alone are in control?

Chapter 4: Teenagers Revealed

Get to know the people behind the transition and watch your teenagers turn into beautiful adults. There are three important areas that you need to be aware of. These areas are what the teenagers consider the most important areas in their lives. Here they are.

Physical Profile

Literally speaking, there is no raising up needed when it comes to physical attributes. Most of them become taller than you, at this time. The completion of secondary sexual characteristics occurs between the mid and the late teens. Right before your very eyes, you can see their bodies transition from being children to adults. However, this is when awkwardness starts. They do not feel comfortable yet with their new bodies. They look lanky and out of proportion and, awkward. The appearance of pimples and body hair begins, and this could be a big deal for them.

You can support your children by informing them ahead of time what to expect in their bodies as they grow into adulthood. At this stage, they will be so preoccupied with their looks. This will become the most important thing for them. This is the time that they will try to fit in with their peers by trying to look like everyone else. They like to follow the trends. They do not want to appear different. And sometimes, this is where the battle begins.

They might want to do something with their hair that you do not approve of. Or buy clothes that you do not like. Pause for a while and think. Is this a battle worth fighting? Choose your battles well. Assess the situation. The best approach is respect, but with compromise. As long as it does not go against your established values, allow them to express their styles. If the changes that they want are not going to harm them physically (like all those piercings in unusual places) or permanently (like tattoos), give them some space and let them be. That pink hair trend would soon disappear.

Tell your teenagers that they are beautiful the way they are, but allow them space to discover that truth for themselves. Asserting themselves to you is one way of establishing their identity. Provide room for growth while keeping things in their proper perspective.

Emotional Profile

They don't call it the stage of the "raging hormones" for nothing. Indeed, this is the time of the roller coaster ride of emotions. Understand that at this stage, the hormones are very active for both genders. There will be mood swings, heavy drama and illogical thoughts and actions. And since this is also the stage where they discover that the opposite sex is a wonderful thing, this is when puppy love and crushes start. And for some parents, this is the start of many sleepless nights, too.

How do you manage the emotional instability of teenagers? Ignoring them can lead to more attention seeking behaviors. Spanking them would cause more harm than good. Threatening them would make rebels out of them. Making fun, or the light of it would widen the gap or distance between you and your teen. The key is proper communication. Talk to them as you would an adult. Know what is important for them, and respect them. Let them know that they can tell you their concerns with you without being judged or scolded.

Most parents are not comfortable discussing sensitive topics with their teens. However, they are going to learn about these things whether it's from you or someone else. Which would you rather have? As Freud theorized, the focus of teenagers usually revolves around their sexuality. They will be curious about so many things regarding sex and sexuality.

Encourage the discussion of sensitive topics like sex or drugs. Be objective and non-malicious when talking about these things. If they cannot get the information from you, they will learn it from their friends and peers, who happen to know nothing about those things in the first place. Having an open line of communication is a good thing to have inside the house. Let your teen know that they can talk to you anytime about anything.

Social Profile

At this stage, the most influential person for them is not you anymore. It is their friends now. As parents, you should not feel threatened that your kids do not look up to you the same way they did when they were younger. It is nothing personal. That is just one way of trying to establish independence. They will want to explore and experiment without you.

What can you do? The best approach is to get to know their friends by letting them come to your house. Some parents are quick to give advice to their kids about who to befriend and who not to befriend.

Do not reject their friends outright without giving them valid reasons. Do not decide which kid is a good friend for your kid based on looks alone. Some kids can look weird, but altogether be a good friend for your teen.

The only time you should put your foot down is when they are obviously in bad company. Otherwise, trust your kids' judgment and decision-making skills. Allow them to choose their friends and to have time with them. Your children are smart, too. They will know which friends are good influences for them.

Do not try to bring yourself to the level of their friends. Do not act like their friends act. You should be friends with your children, but they should know their boundary. They must know the dividing line between being a friend and an authority figure. Your authority as the parents should remain intact. They will sometimes hate you for that but later on, they will appreciate all the time that you went against their will to do your roles as a parent.

These three areas - the physical, the emotional, and the social areas of your teenager's life count the most at this point. Learning to manage these three areas means you are already halfway to winning the battle.

Chapter 5: Spanking And Yelling Are Counterproductive

You are at home and you have told your daughter to do something four times but she is not responding. There is a high probability that the fifth time will not be easy for her. You will either shout or hit her. Not that you are pleased to do it, but because circumstances have forced you to do it. The child will cry and eventually do what you asked. The question is; has it helped her?

You may think you have solved the problem but truth is those methods of instilling discipline do not really work. They only make the child to become aggressive, always anxious, scared and will only do the right thing for the sake of it.

Shouting and spanking are known to solve problems at the moment but cause more harm than good in the long run.

Disadvantages of spanking preschoolers;

·Spanking makes a child to have an aggressive behavior study has shown that children who are often spanked are more aggressive as compared to those who are not spanked.

Punishing is expected to stop terrible conduct in kids, yet a few studies have inferred that it does precisely the opposite. Numerous childcare and brain science specialists assert that punishing just shows a kid that roughness is a worthy type of discipline. On the off chance that a youngster grows up with this mentality, he could use violence to tackle conflicts with age mates when there are more satisfactory methods to resolve them.

·Spanking does not teach respect but fear While beating a youngster is thought by its supporters to be an approach to teach respect, admiration and discipline other individuals say that it shows a kid to fear her parents. Hitting regularly is viewed as a type of misuse; abused casualties live in fear of their abusers. There is little respect and regard in a damaging relationship. The individuals who consider punishing to be a form of abuse say that the children behave well only so that they won't be spanked. They don't take after standards out of emotions of affection and appreciation; they follow rules and regulations out of fear and anxiety. They figure out how to stay away from punishment not because it is important to follow rules.

·Spanking causes danger to both the parent and the child Studies uncover that punishing is risky to kids. Indeed, numerous studies have uncovered that the more folks beat their kids, the more conceivable youngsters are to hit their guardians. This demonstration will really place them in risk for a few issues later in their life. Beating youngsters additionally has potential long haul consequences for some kids. This can trigger animosity, rowdiness, viciousness or even criminal conduct. This may likewise bring about mental issues to kids.

·It undermines trust the special bond between parents and their child is broken. Trust no longer prevails as the young ones are afraid of their parents. They afraid that if they open up their parents may react aggressively.

Children who are spanked are also likely not to trust other people especially older ones.

What is more important than having your child's trust?

· Lower Self-Esteem

As per The Child Mind Institute, shouting at your youngster can make her have low self regard. This is especially genuine if the words you holler at her are particularly harming, for example, "I wish you were never conceived," or, "You'll never add up to anything." Even a basic inquiry yelled in resentment, for example, "Why in the world would you do that?" can hurt your youngster on the grounds that the hidden message in your manner of speaking may be advising her, "I believe you are silly"

· Animosity Hollering at your youngster may make him turn out to be physically forceful, particularly when discussing youthful youngsters. Since he can't generally verbalize his awful sentiments, he'll strike out in the main way that he knows how. This may show in animosity toward you, his companions or other people who are younger than him.

· Poor Modeling shouting at individuals isn't considered a substantial method for managing issues in the grown-up world. For instance, shouting at your manager would presumably get you let go. Yet, kids aren't generally treated with the same appreciation. Kids are extraordinary little imitators, and they're going to emulate your example. In the event that you flip your top at whatever point you get irate, that is the sort of conduct they're going to show when they get furious.

· Consequences for Parents It's not just the kids who are off guard. Folks likewise endure the results of shouting at kids, and it goes well past the daily feeling that you've fizzled presently. It can prompt extra stretch, hypertension and expanded danger of stroke and heart assault. Keeping your cool can enhance your wellbeing.

Chapter 6: Parenting Skills That Will Shape Your Children

Parents are the very first teachers all children have. Parents are solely responsible for beginning the proper steps of raising a child in a healthy environment, to receive the proper education they need and deserve and to provide them with the nutrition they require to grow healthy and strong. Truly effective parenting includes positive attributes that children will soon learn to master. As a parent, you must have particular skills that will positively shape the way your child behaves both in public and behind closed doors.

As parents, we all have a very vital role in the future, for we are literally shaping it through our children. By utilizing positive parenting methods, you are positively shaping the generations of people to come. Whether you like to believe it or not, you are a small part of the future of our world. If anything, history has taught us that without the building of a strong foundation, a child can be led to be confused and lost as they develop. This is why being aware of positive and healthy techniques of parenting are not only good for your child but for your sake too.

Creating Clear Expectations through Communication

In order to be a successful positive parent, one must have some sort of game plan that they will use to discipline their kids when they misbehave. It is only then that your children will learn what you expect from them at all times. But this is not enough. As a parent, you must be willing to model these good behaviors in order for your children to really listen and obey you.

The first step is to discuss your expectations for your children with your partner. You must have a solid front in order to keep your kids from finding loop holes in the boundaries you set. Take the time to really communicate with one another what is expected not only from your kids but from each other as well. Make a list of these expectations. As you do so, think of the various scenarios that you and your kids may experience, and how to discipline them in each one. Remember to take into account the age of your children during this process. Sometimes setting expectations according to age and ability can involve gray areas, so here are three questions to consider:

Have you taught your kids your expectations?

Can they understand the expectations you give them clearly?

Can they perform what is expected of them sufficiently?

Asking yourself these questions can help you to clearly lay out the expectations you desire from each of your kids, no matter their age. Do not expect your four-year-old to whip up dinner and then punish them for not doing as such. That is unrealistic. And you probably will be eating most of that dinner off of the floor anyways.

Once you as parents have set clear and realistic rules and expectations you wish your kids to follow, you will need to effectively communicate them to your child. This is where many parents struggle because they simply either do not know how to communicate with their kids or they do so in such a fashion that their children resist.

For example, your child draws right onto the kitchen counter. Instead of raising your voice and smacking their crayons away from them and sending them to their room, use positive communication. Provide them with calm, positive feedback on what they specifically did wrong and what they should do next time. This will allow the child to really consider the situation and let it sink in, so they learn from their mistakes.

As a parent, you cannot make the rules you make for the household and then proceed to break them constantly. You are the ultimate role model for your child. If you break them, they feel free to do the same. So, in order to keep the peace in the household regarding expectations, stick beside the boundaries that you yourself set. This will help your child see you are a perfect role model for how they should be conducting themselves, both at home and in public.

I cannot express enough the importance of simple communication. In my house, we have family meetings so that we can clearly express the expectations to our kids for that week, etc. This also gives children time to ask questions they are unsure of, which saves a lot of trouble later down the line and from getting your toes stepped on. These meetings have drastically changed my family and assisted in my kids behaving better, for they are not confused, which can result in anger and spite.

Learn to Remain Calm during Chaos

Trust me, when turmoil is in the air, it can be rather easy to get upset and use negative actions that are fueled by negative emotions, especially with children. As a parent, you should expect to have many "off" days where you would rather lock yourself in your bedroom closet and hope the little monsters won't locate your hiding spot. But I have learned the hard way that staying calm, even though much easier said than done, is a lot more effective than getting all worked up over little things. As a parent, you already know that children can be rebellious creatures. This can lead adults to get all caught up in the heat of the moment, resulting in not being able to think properly and saying/doing things we really don't mean. Children are programmed to push limits and your buttons. They are learning which boundaries they can cross. So, it's vital to commonly practice positive thinking and to not take what your children say or do personally. Instead, hone in on behaviors and what is causing them. Always do so in a calm manner. This sense of calm may confuse the child, for as they get older; they are mischievous and do certain things **just** to tick you off. So, don't give them what they want!

Consistency with Consequences

Consequences, both positive and negative, are both equally important to instill in the process of encouraging behaviors from your kids that you desire. When you find your child is doing as they are told or doing something positive on their own accord, you need to utilize positive consequences. Rewards can be small and both short and long term. I recommend using rewards that don't cost a whole lot of money, if any. Creating this sort of reward system can successfully shape any child's behavior. Make a list of un-approving actions and make them clear to them over time. This way, they will want to find more opportunities to obey you more rather than the opposite.

Using negative consequences, on the other hand, can be pretty darn counteractive. It is problematic, since with this system you are adding a negative consequence in order to reduce a certain behavior. But, there is a right way to utilize them. You must have found that a negative consequence can be challenging. This is where the whole remaining calm thing comes in handy. Learn to focus on one particular area in order to get them to behave appropriately. Instead of simply taking away something, take something away from them that is important to them and that they hold dear. Having them perform additional chores and taking away television watching for the evening is a good example of utilizing negative consequences. Your child will then learn to avoid the behavior that made them take out the trash, etc.

But, the kicker to all of this is that both parents must be consistent with the way they utilize positive and negative consequences. Without consistency, your children will learn nothing from what you are trying to instill. Consistency is essentially the backbone of disciplining. Consistency is a trait that all great parents have, since without it, your child can become confused easily.

Be a Good Role Model

"Do what I say and not what I do." Ah, a common thing I am sure you heard as a child yourself. But this phrase is confusing to kids. Children have a funny way of not doing what their parents say, simply because they are modeling what their parents do instead. If your child is somewhat problematic, perhaps it is time to look in the mirror and ask yourself what you might be doing that your child is attempting to mirror. As a parent, a priority should always be to do your best and strive to set a good example for your kids.

This is why role playing during childhood is important, for it's another great technique that teaches your child how to act without having to turn to punishments. While role playing, implement the right practices for the role-playing scenario at hand. This will help your child to see the problem with certain behaviors. There are a few very simple steps any parent can do in order to teach their kids good, healthy behaviors through the means of role playing:

As you role play, occasionally swap roles with your child and allow them to play your part

Set a stage by narrating the scene

Begin role playing

Provide critiques by utilizing positive feedback and praise

Role playing allows your child to ponder over situation in advance and teaches them adaptive responses to scenarios that could be frustrating to them. This allows their mind to become more thoughtful of others, as well as have more flexible responses to everyday issues that they will inevitably face in the future.

Praise Effectively

From parent to parent, we both know the power that praise has. In fact, it is possibly one of the most crucial acts you can perform as a parent. It is the nourishment that allows your kids to grow both emotionally and physically healthy. Praise is a technique that homes in on focusing on situations. Praise lays the foundation for a strong self-esteem so that your child can feel secure in their own skin. Believe it or not, the more praise given, the better behaved your child will more than likely be. It not only encourages good behavior but influences them to do well at the tasks they will face.

Chapter 7: In A Nutshell

If you always do what you've always done you will always get what you've always got.

This is all about:

* recognizing when a pattern of behaviour is not working,

* taking responsibility for changing it,

* you becoming aware that you have choices,

* deciding exactly what you want to happen, visualize it in detail,

* believing that you will get it,

* believing that it has value to you to get it,

* stepping into their shoes to express it in a way that will achieve it,

* noticing what works and repeating it.

Personal note from me...

How often do we as parents get on with our own stuff when the kids are behaving and only give them attention when they are being naughty. Is this a pattern that's likely to result in good behaviour?

Personal note to yourself...(use this space to write any notes about what you'd like to do differently and record how well it goes, what worked best)

What I'd like to do differently is

When I did it, what worked best was

2. You have the resources to do whatever you want to do.

What an amazing thought!

Yes you have a huge number of skills that you have been acquiring since childhood. Each one, when applied in a different context gives you yet more skills and options.

Lots of parents think that they have no skills, especially when things aren't going well, but that is not so. In the hurly burly of parenthood it's easy to feel overwhelmed and feel we can't cope. We spend a lot of our energy making sure the kids have self-esteem and we praise them every day but who praises us?

So if you are feeling a low sense of self-belief like that, imagine that someone else is watching you over the course of the day.

What would they observe?

What would they see you do?

The skills you use automatically or unconsciously may well be skills that other people would wish they had. We tend to take for granted what we do well and feel envious of other parents' skills. Pretend you are someone who doesn't know you, observing all you do.

* What would they observe?

* What skills are you using?

* Write down the skill you use to do that thing. .

What do you believe about doing this thing?

How important is the way you do it?

How well do you feel you do this thing?

Now list each thing you do well and give each one a score out of 10 for how important it is to you to do this thing well.

Ask yourself, 'What does that ALSO mean I can do?'

Write that down in a list here.

………………………………………..

………………………………………..

………………………………………..

………………………………………..

………………………………………..

You may be surprised at how you can use a skill in many different parts of your life. This is such an important concept to pass on to your child.

When they say, "I can't do…" ask them;

* What skill do you think you need to do it?

* Where do you use that skill now, perhaps in a different activity? (you may need to help a younger child become aware of where they use that skill)

* How could you use that skill for this task?

* Imagine how you will feel when you've achieved it? (a young child may want to draw a smiley face or give a thumbs up sign)

Whenever you are struggling:

o Identify the skill you need.

o Think about when and where you had that skill.

o Ask yourself, what was the belief you had that enabled you to use that skill.

o Take on that belief now in order to access the skill.

When we talk about taking on a belief in NLP we mean that we change our belief.

A belief is not a value. A value is a code you live by and that is not likely to change as it is instilled in you as a child and is governed by both your upbringing and your environment.

A BELIEF is something you hold about the things you do and changes as you experience new situations and people.

For example, you certainly hold different beliefs now from those you held as a child such as believing in Father Christmas or the Tooth Fairy!

Our beliefs about parenthood will have changed as a result of becoming a parent and continue to change as you talk to other parents, read magazines and articles on the Internet and as your children grow up.

When your child does something you don't like, do you feel you're a failure?

THIS IS A limiting belief.

You are not a failure. What you are doing simply isn't working so do something different.

Notice when they do what they are told, what did you do differently on that occasion?

You do have the skill. We can be inclined to generalize, distort and delete.

We say, "You NEVER do what you're told." That's just not true, is it? It's a generalisation. We may also distort or mind-read by saying to ourselves that they are deliberately trying to annoy us or that this means that we are bad parents.

Do we also delete those times when they have done what we asked?

Check your language patterns and avoid generalisations, distortions and deletions. These are filters that get in the way of clear communication and tend to create limiting beliefs that sometimes stay with us and prevent us from being the best we can be.

Chapter 8: Raise Your Teenager Properly Through Conscious Parenting

With the gradual growth of your toddler to a teenager, it demands effective growth of conscious parenting as well. Due to enormous biological and intellectual changes taking place in the mind and body of your child, it is obvious that they face various emotional and psychological conflicts. Raising a teenager through conscious parenting is also not at all difficult. It only requires you to treat your teenager child as an individual and not as an obedient brood.

The parents are essentially required to learn and understand the distinctive shades of teenage conduct as well as the outstanding strategies of prevention to not let your child grow far away from you on a risky and transitory path. This is considered to be the most crucial stage of development where the teenagers generally oscillate between the good world and the bad world due to which they usually act unpredictably. In order to handle efficiently this unpredictable mind with the help of conscious parenting, it is essential to understand some crucial dilemmas and confusions of a teenager. Some of the significant ways to handle the teenagers include –

Maintain the integrity of the Bond

The phase of a teen is essential from numerous perspectives. The bond between the parents and the child becomes delicate and if the parents fall short inunderstanding their feelings and neglect them, this bond of mutual understanding may begin todisintegrate. Thus it is very much essential to understand the psyche and state of your child from the beginning as a conscious parent which will ensure outstanding strength to the bond. In the event that you have recently understood the significance of parenting consciously, you require putting in all your best efforts to keep your bond secure. Try to spend plenty of time with your teenage kid and involve yourself in their activities to remain close to them. You can make it necessary to have one time meal together in the family to keep the cohesiveness of the family intact.This will help in maintaining the closeness in relationship.

Residingas one

With the growth of your kid as a teenager, a significant notion of being an outcast generally gets developed in the mind of the parents due to which they reduce the interaction with them. However, conscious parenting supportsthe fact of remaining close and united with your kid even at the time of their teenage years. It requires huge amount of flexibility among parents to understand the thoughts and ideas of their young teenagers. It is essentially required to pay undivided attention to the thoughts and ideas of your child which will ensure a unified bond of closeness between you and your child. Take out significant amount of time from your regular busy routine to spend with your child and try to make that time duration fun filled for themby thinking of significant ways to enhance the interactions.

Bridging the gap of opinions

One interesting fundamental of teenage life is they always consider your opinion to be futile for them. Your right may be their wrong....and vice versa. This would require understanding the mind and the mindset of your child in a conscious way. Consider that the times are changing and as a parent you have to be closer to your teenager. Estimate the interest of your teenager and learn their style. Be innovative and work towards to know how to break ice without trying too hard. Keep an easy-going demeanor to develop a positive attitude.

Understand Your Teenager

As a conscious parent, understand the growing children and make this transition hassle free. There may be a string of pressures faced by teens ranging from peer pressures to performance anxiety. Teens struggle hard to switch from being dependent to being independent, with many changes to be taken in their stride. These are the years the teens struggle real hard to assert their individuality. Make your child feel good and that would immediately reflect back.

Make sure you start this task much earlier by - Maintaining a loving home environment; establishing atmosphere of trust, respect and honesty; allowing appropriate independence; encouraging interaction and communication; inculcating a sense of sharing and responsibility.

Understanding Teenage Boys

Don't feel shocked if video games, friends, and the occasional sports practice are fast replacing by sports, video games, finding an image, friends, experiencing new things, and girls in your teenage son's life. Your young boy may seem terse and uncommunicative. Just understand that he is managing to deal with his share of workload. Actually, he's just getting attuned to this new train of thoughts. He's not upset with you or getting indulged into a rebellious phase.

If your son is trying to act smart allow him to be. He is in the phase where he is seeking validation from his peers. You may think it to be pointless, but he does not. And he won't be able to see it despite your efforts. Instead of lecturing him on the pitfalls of society, steer him in a productiveand safedirection consciously.

Some more tips for parenting teenager boys are -

o Be the one to show him the world and help him develop his own personality. Introducing him to your world is a good place to start.

o   Don't force down the knowledge or learning and show him different sports, forms of art and expression, different foods, outside activities, past times, and new people and places. Allow him to get a sense of self coming defiantly from you.

o   Whenever your son tries to convey his feelings, don't dismiss. If your son actually takes the time to open up don't look at him like the naive, inexperienced kid that he is. After all, you were in the same boat years ago.

o   Don't snigger unnecessarily. He's going to make mistakes in order to grow up. Encourage him to explore his feelings and advise in a subtle way. Be like a rock he can lean on.

o   Expect that your son will explore the world of porn. This isn't alarming. It's normal. Do initiate a conversation on the topic, letting him know that what he's seeing isn't realistic. Ground him in reality in a friendly way.

o Help your son in exploring his maturity. Treat him like an adult at home and he won't feel the need as much to prove himself around you and his friends. Make him part of plans, problems, and other associated issues.

o Your teenage son may use more foul language, address you rudely, and demand more independence. Now, here act smartly. If he desperately wants to be grown up, give him responsibilities.

o Meet your son's friends. Get into his world by meeting his friends. Tell him they can come over and know his social circle better. Initially, your son and his friends may be a little wary to come home, but you have to earn their trust for this.

o   Set a good example for your teenager. Using your cell phone at the dinner table is telling him to talk on his cell phone at the dinner table. If you want him to be an involved part of your life, you'll have to be a part of his. You may feel like he's not paying attention to you, but he is.

o   Your teenage son is going through a lot of things that he may not understand. So initiate meaningful conversation. Even if he can't give you a good answer, you'll get him thinking about it.

If your teenager wants to go for an outlandish hair cut or a dress, consider it's not the end of the world. Remember all those eccentric demands you made to your parents. It's the same thing happening in a cyclic way. However, if your child is showing negative signs that are out of character, you may need to take action.

Keep a vigilant eye for-Weight loss or gain; Less or excessive sleeping; Drastic changes in personality; Change in social circle; Skipping school continually; Poor and inconsistent grades; Suicidal tendencies, etc.

If you notice any of these, contact a psychologist. These could be warning signs to some bigger issue.

Understand Your Teenage Daughter

Every teenage girl may not be as rude or nasty as you may fathom to be. While we as parents may miss hearing every detail of their school day and activities, teenage girls like to keep some things to them. That may hurt but actually they confide in their friends, instead of us. This is just part of the independence process and you just need to allow them to draw some boundaries.

It's also about hormonal changes. Stay prepared for they would make some mistakes. Lectures and warningsmay stop them temporarily. But rest assured, mistakes will be made -- just different ones.

As modern and conscious parents, understand that she needs independence. Don't make all decisions for her. Don't tell her how to do everything. Just back off. In some cases you should tell them what to do, but never over exercise your powers. Love them, support them and let them make mistakes.

You may start believing that your teen daughter hates you, but don't take it to heart. Instead, learn how to decipher her behavior. Understand their feelings on how much control she wants from you. Her brain is developing and she is going through hard times.

One of the best ways to teach your young daughter is by example. So if you break a rule that you make your daughter follow, she will lose respect for both you and the rule.

Respect the identity of your daughter. If she will not get the respect, independence and support, it could lead to depression. Respect your teenage daughter so that she respects you in return. You need to show her what respect is first. She must already be very insecure in dealing with the pressures and struggles of growing up. So just be careful in handling her.

Don't be judgmental and refrain from emotional abuse. Tell your daughter she is beautiful just the way she is, since her own insecure thoughts are telling her otherwise.Your teenage daughter is growing up now and changing. Let her know that you aren't just a nagging parent; and want the best for her. Let her think of you as a friend she can confide in.

And some other ways to handle her —

·Just talk to her and tell her that you are there to help. Don't sound overprotective. She carries a personal life that she cannot surrender on that front. Just stay patient.

·Give her responsibilities and respect her wishes. Allow her to have some uninterrupted time alone. Your behavior with her should be less restrictive.

·Don't expect your teenage daughter to fully and happily obey your commands. Your commands should come backed with reason or explanation.

·Convey that you truly love her and that youdon't want to just restrict or boss her around. Let her know that you love her.

Chapter 9: Common Parenting Challenges In The Tech Era

Our fast paced, technology-centered era has changed society a lot over the past few years, bringing with it many parenting challenges. The pressure on parents has always been the same, but nowadays the era of technology has dynamically changed the way people are bringing up children. New parenting challenges keep parents on their toes all the time, which is why positive parenting solutions are such a valid resource for parents who struggle with obstacles on a daily basis. Only the parents can help themselves overcome these challenges and transition themselves and their children from a negative to a positive attitude.

Parents must be proactive in raising their children, staying aware of the challenges today's generation faces on a day to day basis, and combating problems with patience, respect, and unconditional love. Here are just a few of the issue both parents and children face:

• Balancing Parenthood and Career

Because both parents often have to work nowadays to maintain a good lifestyle, it gets difficult to manage time with your child. Parents cannot be present in the here and now because they have to focus on the long-term aspects of saving for their child's future or simply getting by month to month. The parent's absence is not something the child understands, which creates misunderstandings and fills the child with negative feelings. This can eventually have an effect on the parent-child relationship and cause any sense of closeness to erode over time. That's why it is important for parents to find a balance between parenthood and their career. Remember, your child is only young once. Never let work overtake special time with your child and be sure that even when you are absent, your child knows that you love them and care about them.

- Discipline Maintenance

To properly discipline your child, you have to spend time with them on a daily basis so the child can learn little actions of life which you do not teach verbally but demonstrate through action.

- Encouragement from Parents

When parents are busy with their careers, the child misses out on encouragement. This can foster a sense of low self-esteem in the child as well as self-doubt. They will struggle with making their own decisions and will not seek out independence like they should because their confidence was not boosted at the right time.

- Time Is More Important Than Things

Some parents try to replace their absence with things to keep their child happy. But time will always be far more valuable to the child than things. Whenever possible, give your child your time. Giving your time allows the child to know they are important and loved.

Sometimes parents believe they have to work all the time to provide nice things for their child. But you have to weigh the cost of your absence. While you are gone, your child misses you and feels sad about not getting to spend time together. The sadness and lack of interaction as a family can affect their behavior, and eventually, they might distance themselves from any sort of deep bond with you, causing a distant relationship that cannot be repaired.

- Meeting Expectations of Children

When a child demands something and parents are not able to fulfill it due to their busy schedule, it can cause a string of negative emotions in the child. They might not understand why you can't take time to go to the park or watch a movie with them. They might feel like all you care about is work and that they always come last. This can cause not only behavioral problems, but a lack of respect as well. After all, if it seems as if you don't have time to consider their needs, then why should they care about yours? That's why it is so important for parents to put themselves in their child's shoes. Try to understand where you child is coming from and always ensure they understand how important they are in your life. Talk to your kids, make special plans with them when you are able to set aside time, and make an effort to be a part of their day to day life as much as you can.

- Technology and Your Child

Technology is a part of everyone's life nowadays. It's hard to keep a child away from an iPad, TV, computer, phone and more when you are away at work. When they feel lonely, children will often turn to gadgets to help them pass the time. But don't be fooled into thinking gadgets can replace your responsibility as a parent. Only you can provide the foundation and unconditional love a child needs to thrive.

Chapter 10: Always Tell The Truth

At any age honesty is the best policy. When children are very young, they do not know how to tell a lie, but this can change quickly as they develop. No parent wants their children to tell 'fibs', but if you catch them telling a fib, how you react will start to shape their future responses both to you and others.

If a room is a mess and nothing is put away, or something is broken, some children may deny it was them. They may blame their sibling or a friend or even one of the pets. You clearly know it was your child and not the excuse they are offering. They may continue with their explanation which you know is not true. You could stop them and tell them that you know they are not telling you the truth. Another recommended approach is to stop them and ask them to think again. "Are you sure that is what happened?" Allow for long pauses if there is no immediate response. Reassure them that you are not going to be upset at them, but it is important that they tell you the truth. It is crucial that you are calm in your tone and behavior. With this, you can generally get the child to tell you what happened. If you are elevated in your tone, or you become emotional, then the child may become upset, and you will be less likely to get them to open up.

It is important to talk to children about why they lied and what the consequences could be. By talking calmly to them about the reasons why they lied versus just punishing them for lying will help their behavior in the future.

Once they have told you the truth, you should praise the child for being honest, and you should thank them. This does not mean they should escape being punished; which should be whatever you consider reasonable to show them that there are consequences to lying and bad behavior. Perhaps missing a play date or withholding video games for a period of time as an example, but the honesty should be praised. Reward positive behavior with praise.

There is no greater coaching than leading by example. Your children need to see that you are honest. Many people are guilty of telling the occasional white lie, and they don't consider a white lie to be a true lie. To a child, a lie is a lie, and if your children see you telling lies, they will not be able to distinguish between a 'white lie' and an 'out and out' lie. You may have a good reason for the lie, but it is important not to engage even in a white lie in front of your children.

If your child hears you telling a friend over the phone, you don't feel well, which is why you are not going to a social function, when the truth is you don't feel like it, and your child can see you are perfectly fine, this is not setting the right example and causes confusion. The example you are setting is that there are times you can lie if it suits you. This is not a lesson that we want our children to learn. They may even ask you, "don't you feel well Mommy?" This has the potential for you to add to the initial 'white lie' or defend your 'white lie' as justified. Either will further add to the child's confusion. Children need situations to be black or white at these critical developmental and foundational years, so they have clarity in how they should behave. Seeing this demonstrated by you shows them exactly how to behave.

Building self-esteem

Self-esteem is a child's emotional evaluation of what they think they are worth and how good they feel about themselves. Research has shown a child's self-esteem is a predictor of future outcomes such as academic achievement, social interactions, overall health, fitness and well-being. Children with higher self-esteem are more confident and generally happier than other children.

Low self-esteem will affect a child's schooling and can carry into adulthood, possibly impacting future job performance and having a negative impact on their personal relationships. Providing positive reinforcement is an easy way to start to develop high self-esteem for your child. Learning to ride a bike, getting a good grade on a school assignment, or coloring a picture without going outside the lines are simple examples where you can provide positive reinforcement that will build self-esteem.

You should never compare the skills and progress of your child to another child as this can build negative self-esteem. Your child's skills and accomplishments should be only compared to themselves. As an example, last week they could just swim three strokes, but this week they swam half way across the pool. It does not matter if other children can swim all the way across the pool. Positively reinforce the huge progress that your child has made, and they will feel great about their progress and achievements and want to do more.

Always recognize the effort not the result. Knowing that your child worked hard on a homework assignment but did not get a good grade, you should positively recognize the effort that they put it. "I am so proud of how hard you worked on that assignment."

Above all, never allow negative statements as they can sometimes become self-fulfilling prophecies. "I knew I wasn't going to make the team." This should be addressed by promoting the positive achievements of the child. "You are great at sports. You work really hard and just need to spend a little more time practicing, and you will do better next time."

Your example of how you behave in front of your children will always have a great influence on how they behave throughout their lives. If you are positive and constantly looking at the bright side of any situation, it will help the child to emulate you. If they did not make the try outs at the school basketball team, instead of disappointment you may hear them say, "I am going to practice hard and try again next season."

Praise builds self-esteem and motivates children to excel

Young children can get bored quickly, and they need to be constantly challenged to help with their development and to build self-esteem. Children need to be challenged with more and more complex tasks. They also need to be encouraged to complete any task to the best of their abilities. It is one thing to clean your room by putting everything in one drawer and forcing it to shut, and another to fold the clothes nicely and put each back in its correct spot. Coloring a picture is great, but as skills develop the coloring should improve and the child should be continuously praised for getting better at coloring with more difficult pictures.

Children love to be praised and recognized, but the praise should be elevated when the task is completed at a higher level. "Thank you for cleaning your room" versus, "you did a fantastic job on cleaning your room. I see you folded all your clothes and put each one back in its proper spot. You shut all the drawers and even put away your homework. I am very proud of you, great job."

This type of positive reinforcement will build self-esteem and encourage the child to not only complete tasks, but complete them to the best of their ability. Continuing to challenge the child with different tasks will set those foundational skills that will help them excel.

Chapter 11: Hold A Family Meeting Every Week

Holding a family meeting every week right from the start is the best idea ever! What will this do for your new blended family? You will be amazed how these meetings will be the glue to pull your family together and help to keep it together.

What exactly should happen at this meeting? This gathering should take place every single week. Sundays are probably the best time to hold your meetings. Usually the children will be at home because of school on Monday. The best place to gather is at the kitchen or dining room table. Everyone should be sitting up and not lounging or slouching on a sofa or the floor.

The first topic should be "how was your week?" Each member should have AT LEAST one comment to make. For every negative comment that is made, there should be a positive comment. Hold to this rule. It proves that there are some positive things that are happening in their lives. When we focus and discuss only the negatives of a situation, the tone of the meeting will be negative no matter how hard you try to change it.

Who should go first? Make it vary. Change the order every week. One week, start with the oldest and go down to the youngest; the next week, do the opposite. Use alphabetical order, using the first initial of their first or middle names. Go by the month of their birthdays. Be creative with order.

When a child states a negative, put everyone in charge with coming up with a solution until the issue is addressed and he or she is satisfied with a solution. Then this child must state a positive, and everyone offers support or praise. When the children are finished, then the parents share their thoughts. The same rule applies to the parents. You must have one positive for every negative. This shows the children how important each one of their roles is in building this blended family.

After the issues are all addressed, then it is time to discuss the week ahead. There should be a large calendar—one of the big desk calendars works really well for this step. Each child will report to mom or dad what obligations he or she has for the week. This is a good way to be sure that all children will be able to get to wherever they need to go for school and extracurricular activities. Being organized and informed helps things to run most smoothly.

When a family grows quickly in size, there are so many things that need to be addressed. These things can cause huge problems when they pop up at the last minute. This calendar must be used respectfully; for example, one person can not write really big and not allow enough space for others. Perhaps each child could have a different color ink to write down his or her activities. Or the parent can do the writing.

This meeting will be a place where each person can be heard and have their problems addressed with the other members of the family. Also, sharing successes can help to show a sense of pride in each other. Issues communicated to the whole family can become easily solved when more "heads" think on them and offer solutions.

Be consistent with the meeting and the rules of the meeting. It is not to be a complaint session only—that is why there must be a positive for every negative. Make your family a democratic family—where every person's thoughts and ideas are welcomed and respected.

Chapter 12: How To Stop Shouting At The Child?

Sometimes, even the most loving parents lose their temper. Many moms and dads raise their voices because they are '**programmed**' to shout – their parents did it. Some of them let themselves yell at the child only in cases when they are too upset or angry. Think about the fact that shouting hurts the kid's self-esteem and destroys the spiritual relation between him and you.

When parents shout, children become frightened. They take shouting as an attack. Consequently, they either rush to the fight (snarling at us and shouting in response) or run away, trying to get away from screaming, physically or emotionally.

Children learn how to communicate by imitating our manner of communication. If we intentionally scream at the child to make him do what we want, this is called bullying. And children learn to shout at others to force them to do what they need to be done. If adults scream at the child unintentionally, it means that they have lost control. And the child realizes that shouting at the others is an entirely appropriate way to deal with a bad mood. The shouting problem can be removed, and the emotional harm caused by it can be reduced.

New skills

Tell your child that you'll try to pull yourself together to stop shouting at him, and ask him to help you. Permit him to interrupt you when you start crying. Offer some pantomime, like covering ears with palms. Moreover, shouting can be interrupted with the words, **'You're shouting at me, and I am unpleased**,' or **'Please talk to me quietly, because you love me.'**

React to this reminder by using the technique of **'rewind, setting, and restart.'**

Example:

Rewind. 'Thank you for reminding me, I forgot about this, because I was upset.'

Setting. "I'm sorry, you don't deserve to be shouted at. What you have done is not good, but I shouldn't have shouted at you anyway.'

Restart. 'Let's start it anew. I am upset because you don't agree with me.'

Our permission to children to remind us that we shouldn't shout:

- gives them the power to protect themselves from crying without starting the fight (not escaping);

- protects their self-esteem, for it lets them understand that they don't deserve such treatment;

- strengthens the relationship, for we express our respect for their needs and feelings.

Chapter 13: Examples Of Good Parenting

We live in a world where satisfying the voice that says "I want" often becomes the dominant behavior. Even as adults, there are many who put themselves before their children. It is about what they want or desire versus what is good for their children. We also have the desire for instant gratification or the need to "have it now". Credit card companies make their living off of this impulse.

Once again, you need to lead by example. It is always better to buy only what you can afford rather than use a credit card and this is something you should do in front of your child. Practicing self-control in front of your child can be an important lesson and a great example of positive parenting.

To do this, go to an ATM and pull out the cash you need for the activity you are doing. You want to be positive, but you also want to start teaching budgets as you provide a positive environment.

Try to start using statements like, "I wanted to bring you here for the fun and enjoyment of it. I think there is more value in spending time together than any toy I could buy you because in a few years, you'll grow out of the toy and it won't be as meaningful as the memories." This statement is positive and shows your child that you value their company over material items.

Here are some suggestions for going places and how to handle requests for souvenirs. These tips will also help if your child wants to do more than one planned activity a day:

Tell your child exactly what the day will entail.

Explain you have budgeted for the activity.

Tell your child that you wish to spend time with them and show them something new.

Remind your child that the memory they will have of the activity is more important.

Another option, if you do decide to buy a souvenir, is to explain to your child that you'll stop at the gift shop once you have completed your outing but that stopping in the gift shop does not mean you will definitely buy something. Tell your child you will consider making a purchase; however, they have to give you one reason why they like that toy versus something they already have.

Be sure to explain that just because you go into the gift shop it does not mean you will make a purchase. You are not going to get a toy just because it is expected, but rather because there is something they are truly interested in owning.

Finally, you need to tell your child before you go on your outing that you will base any souvenir purchase on their behavior during the day. If they spend the day complaining or misbehaving, then you may need to avoid the gift shop all together.

Providing the Right Examples of Respectful, Loving, Understanding Behavior

Throughout the book, you have learned how your behavior can influence your children, but there are other ways your children can be influenced. One of these are the individuals you allow in your child's life. In fact, the people, peers or even the

TV your child watches can have a significant impact.

As the parent, you will need to provide good examples of love, respect, and understanding through more than just you and your spouse. This includes the type of media you allow into your child's life.

TV shows will need to be chosen based on what they provide. Choose shows that fit your child's age and avoid allowing access to shows that are for older children. For example, teen programs for an eight-year-old will not provide the right lessons and your child will not be able to understand the lessons the show has.

You will also want to limit access to the internet or monitor their internet usage. Some websites such as YouTube should be restricted unless your child is using the videos to learn how to do something such as a craft. Of course, books are another option for learning as well but be sure to provide the right choices there too.

To find the right books for your child, go to a bookstore and ask the store clerk about popular selections for children in your child's age group. You can also look at books on topics your child is interested in, for example, if they like the stars you can buy a book geared towards astronomy and so on. Picking a book with a subject that your child already enjoys sets yourself up to succeed and help your child learn.

Community Involvement

Your children should be involved in the community as soon as possible. Community involvement means going to boy or girls clubs, participating in girl or boy scouts or through other ways. It is important to expose your child to other adults and children, but be sure these groups have similar values to help your child gain the love, respect, and understanding you wish them to have.

Chapter 14: Dealing With Temper Tantrums

Choosing worthy alternative methods for correcting the child is more helpful than spanking or losing your temper. Don't conquer battles that you can avoid with a bit of persistence and a caring approach. It doesn't always need to be a time-out in the corner of the room. Why not try one of these three methods the next time your toddler throws a tantrum?

Method 1: Discover the Need

Each behavior displayed by a child thrives on needs. Would you punish a child for being tired, hungry, or lonely? Is there too much commotion or too many people around the child causing an upsetting situation? Is there a change in his/her diet, allergies, or illness that could be causing the outbursts?

You need to discover what triggered the crying or tantrum. Attempt to take care of the need. Then, for future incidents, you may have a better way to accommodate the issue without additional drama.

The cure could be as simple as changing the feeding time or having a nap. Changes in a routine can have a definite effect on a child and his/her emotions.

Method 2: Observe the Actions

You need to discover why the child is acting in an unacceptable manner. Ask yourself if any of his/her friends moved away or has someone done something to upset the child. The behavior may not be acceptable, but you need to understand the reason the child is acting out and throwing a tantrum. Try not to use guilt but make an attempt to let the child know if his/her actions could hurt other people.

Let the toddler know it is not a good idea to leave toys in the middle of the floor. It can hurt anyone who steps or slips on them. Join in the child and help pick up the mess. By working on the disaster together, you will teach the child a bit of discipline without raising your voice. Teamwork is essential when raising a child, no matter how old the child is at the time problems are encountered.

Try using an ABC log/chart which is described as follows:

(A) Antecedent: What happened to trigger the behavior?

(B) Behavior: What happened?

(C) Consequence: What is the result of the behavior?

After you have logged a few of the problems, it should become understandable whether there is a pattern of misbehavior. If your child has more than one caregiver, it is important for each person to record these occurrences. An older sibling can also help with the process. In some cases, the child will provide a pattern that can be followed after a few hours, but others could take more time.

Method 3: Fight or Flight

If a child has acted out in the heat of the moment—and they do—it is advisable to love and nurture the child until a calmer attitude ensues. Instead of a time out, take a time-in with your child. Make a conscious effort to be gentle until the child and you have a moment to decide how to fix the problem.

If you aren't quite feeling the mood, begin by thinking of a favorite outing you had with the child. The child will pick up on the renewed pattern as you relax and also become relaxed.

Method 4: Reassess the Request

Small children and toddlers can push the buttons and make you want to demand corrective actions immediately. Is it essential to do the deed right now or have it done your way? Maybe the toys won't be in the exact space where they belong, but maybe the child is remodeling his/her space.

Be sure your child understands what is being asked by you. Sometimes a parent will believe the adolescent will know how to comply with requests. Other times, a child might not comprehend the request because like other life skills, the child will need to learn or grow into the desired behavioral pattern.

Offering to assist is a compromise that will help get the job done without the additional drama. However, by supporting the child's autonomy and limiting your input, you will provide a baseline for a better academic and emotional outcome. After all, it is just a few toys!

SOLVE the Problem

Your toddler might not always be able to make his/her objections evident during a tantrum. Therefore, it is up to you as the parent to get the situation under control and discover a resolution. Use SOLVE to aid in the process:

(S) Separate your emotions.

(O) Offer full attention to the problem.

(L) Listen to all of the information your child has to say or mimic (depending on his/her age).

(V) Validate his/her feelings by adding your idea of the problem or issue.

(E) Empower and allow your child to help solve the problem and try not to rush the process.

Walk Away

You have heard the saying; ignore the small stuff, and that certainly applies to a toddler. If you don't add fuel to the fire, it might burn out, right? At first, a child might get louder or even have more tantrums. As time passes, and the demand doesn't work; it will probably stop.

At any rate, your goal is accomplished, and you are attempting to break the chain. If you are calm and ignore the outburst, the child will probably calm down much quicker. You are holding the power when you push the ignore button. If you engage in the argument or disagreement, you are giving the power to your toddler. Remain consistent and don't give in!

Diversion is Powerful

Toddlers have a short attention span which can give you the deviation necessary to defuse any disagreeable moments or temper tantrums. Find something different to talk about, so he/she forgets what the original tantrum was about, and move onto the next item of the day. Try going into another room away from the area where the outburst began.

As a parent, you need to provide appropriate distractions when your cute kid throws a fit of temper. If a ball was thrown in the house, see if your youngster wants to go outside and throw the ball. Act quickly, and have another activity for the child. Unfortunately, if your options expire, it could be time for another type of break.

Time-Out

Many people use a time-out zone for youngsters who won't adhere to different strategies of discipline to confirm the effectiveness of the desired plan. You must clinch the behavior within the buds, whether or not it is dangerous or aggressive behavior (such as a tantrum). It's essential to let your child know ahead of the time of an incident where the location will be for misbehavior.

Choose several behaviors that could warrant a time out:

Throwing a temper match

Yelling angrily at others

Hitting others

Biting others

If your child acts out using these behaviors, it is important to place him/her in the time-out area immediately. Don't wait to finish a favorite television show or finish the laundry. By the time your chore is completed, the child might not recall what the reasoning was for sitting in the time-out zone.

By the time your kid is approximately two years old, the sitting in time-out theory can be a welcomed release. The time-out method usually works best with younger children (two-year-olds), especially if the child sees the separation as deprivation from the parent.

Choose a less desirable space for the child to occupy for a specified time such as a playpen, a corner, or a chair. Select an area where the child doesn't have any entertainment, but can be safe. If you aren't at home, you can use a car seat as the time-out chair.

Don't appear to be angry (keep your cool), but simply guide your child to the area and demand he/she will stay there until the misbehavior dissipates or until you say he or she can go play again. For younger children, you should be brief (one minute for each year of age).

Ignoring is a good policy while your child is receiving a time-out, but you still need to listen close by and use a timer. The time should begin once the child has calmed down. If the child attempts to leave the space, you can always restart the timer. If your child is old enough to understand the timer, let him/her see it while the time ticks away.

Don't mention the incident after the time-out that placed the youngster into the chair, but find a way to reinforce the child's good behavior at a later time during the day.

If the time-out is successful, your child's feelings or self-esteem is not damaged, in spite of the intense reaction or outburst of attitude. In many cases, the parent might decide the process isn't working and remove the child from time-out status too soon. Early removal is not always a good idea if your child is aware of how much time is left in the corrective seat. The parent's inability to handle the situation efficiently could be a reason the break won't work.

Once again, not everyone believes a time-out is a good way to perform child discipline. It might make the child believe the negative consequence means he/she is bad instead of promoting good behavior.

After the Punishment

Once you have provided appropriate discipline for your toddler, let it stop there. Move on after the time-out or another method is completed. Don't ask for an apology but give the child a hug and let him/her return to a fun-filled day of playtime.

Negative Discipline

Many parents—especially parents from previous generations—believe toddlers can receive a little slap on the bottom or hand if a child is creating a disturbance. It is not always best for history to repeat itself. As a child matures, the slap will probably progress to paddling which will bring more frustration to an already agitated child.

It isn't advisable to use shock and fear as a training tool for a youngster. It doesn't provide any educational value. Children need to understand what is right and wrong, but it doesn't need to be through pain. The power of suggestion can go a lot further to create a tranquil environment and is a lot less stressful than the additional drama of paddling the child.

Discipline is a tool to teach good behavior, but paddling sends the wrong message. Paddling your child can lead to aggressive behavior and can borderline with child abuse if tempers go too far. Spanking can also cause the child to believe it is okay to harm other people that he/she loves or another playmate.

Chapter 15: Make Time For Your Child

We all know how busy life can get sometimes and we do our best to manage all the responsibilities and tasks we need to accomplish on a weekly basis. Your children should obviously be a priority on your list. We drive them to their sports practices and games, drop them off at friend's house or at school, and teach them how to make their bed. At the end of the day, although you have done a lot for them, do you ever feel that you have not had enough time to connect with them or pay them the attention they need? If this is how you feel, it's imperative that you correct this situation, because your children probably feel it too and might resent it.

Your child needs to know you are available for them—if they come back from a friend's house and want to tell you all about the Lego space ship that they built, you should make time to listen. If possible, you should stop what you are doing, sit down and listen to them. Ask questions, be interested and present, and praise them for their accomplishment. If you are going to be busy working around the house, cleaning the garage or working on the computer, let your children know that you are there for them if they need you. As they grow older, children will naturally detach themselves and be more independent. Soon enough you will regret not making enough time for them earlier on.

You should create opportunities to connect with your child and spend time with them. If you are dropping off or picking up your child for school, this is a great time to chit chat. If you are confined in the car for 15-20 minutes twice a day, why not use that precious time to talk to your child about what's going on with their life and show them you care. Don't turn on that talk radio show, instead engage your child with whatever you can think of to talk about. Let him pick the topic, or plan ahead of time some questions to ask him about school. Anything to get the lines of communication open. Or tune in to a radio show you both like to listen to and create a discussion around it. You might even stop for ice cream on the way home once in a while to change up the routine and spend additional time connecting with your son or daughter.

A lot of people use the concept of quality time with their children to avoid having to be more involved on a regular basis. This is not a good practice to adopt. You can't limit your interaction with your child to once a week and expect to develop a healthy and trusting relationship. You have to show them consistency. Remind yourself daily to review your priorities. If you are very busy for a period of time, explain this to your child, so they don't feel left out. You can even involve them in your activities if possible. When you are spending time with your children, try to turn off your phone if possible and stay away from distractions. This is not only teaching them that they are very important to you, but also teaching them to turn off their own electronic devices when spending time with a loved one. Meal times should also be a special time where the family reunites for a half an hour or so. It should be a relaxed period where everyone feels free to talk about their day, their worries or their joys. Bedtime can also be a time that you cherish with your children. Read them a story, have them read you a story or tell each other a joke.

If you have more than one child, make sure you try to divide your attention and time equally. Create some special moments for one on one time with each child. Organize a Mom and daughter day or a Father and Son day, and then reverse it once in a while. When you are talking to your child, or they are telling you a story, don't interrupt them and make sure they know that they have your full attention by making eye contact as you speak to them. Children who are lacking attention, will most likely seek attention in negative ways. They will want to associate with anyone who gives them the attention they are craving, even if these people are not reliable. So be sure to provide them the positive attention they need. The small things you do on a regular basis with your children will matter much more than the trip to Disney World once a year.

It's a great idea to surprise your child on occasion. Write a cute note in their lunch box or give them a coupon for a play date if they show great manners at their grandparent's house. Decorate their pancakes with smiley faces or let them decorate the cupcakes with you. Stop off for an ice cone on a hot summer day on your way home from day care. These special moments you create with them can turn out to be the greatest memories that they will cherish forever.

Chapter 16: Focus On Education

Good parenting does not only involve disciplining your children from birth to adolescence and facing different problems, may it be big or small, as a family. It also includes your responsibility to send your children to good schools, whether privately run, a public institution or home school. And a good parent will strive hard enough to send his or her child to the best school from primary grade until college.

As parents, you want to see your children succeed in school and develop their full potentials to the best of their abilities. You do not want to settle for less when it comes to your children's schooling. You want what is best for them and supporting them all the way will definitely strengthen your bond with your kids.

The big question is, how can you help your children succeed in school? There is a simple answer to that question and that is no other than parental involvement. Over 50 research studies in the United States have concluded that as long as parents get involved with their child's schooling, this will significantly benefit all parties concerned.

Schools drastically improve, not just through their teaching methods, but with regards to facilities present in the institute. With parents like you getting involved with the teachers and school administrators, they get a sense of pressure to perform better because they are trying to gain approval from you. Thus, helping your child to be better too.

Your child directly benefits from your parental involvement in their school years. This is because once you get involved in their schooling, they become more motivated and inspired to do better in class because they know that you are carefully watching them behind their backs. This sets a certain pressure, which is good for your child, to perform better in all aspects of their educational life. This allows them to improve their behavior in and out of the classroom and to meet their diverse needs to better perform in class. All in all, parental involvement significantly increases the scores and performance of their kids, leading them to succeed not only in school but also in life in the long run.

In doing so, such kind of parents consider their child's education to be their own personal responsibility and not the school's. This simply implies that parents who are involved do not rely simply on the school alone to get their kids educated in life. They make it a point that they get involved as much as they can in order to see through the learning process that their kids go through, thus helping them succeed in life.

However, it does not mean that parents devalue the capacity of the teachers to teach their children all the things they need to know about everything in life. They treat teachers and other school personnel as helpers in meeting the educational goals that they want their child to achieve in the long run. Parents provide additional academic enrichment opportunities for their children that nobody else can give.

In related ways, as a parent, it is important to always remember that you are the primary source of information of your child's education. You are the primary instructor who guides and directs your child, whether at home or in school. That is how it should be and achieving this will surely be good for your child's future.

In order to constantly keep you in check for this immense task, you should have a checklist of things you need to do in order to constantly get involved with your child's schooling. The first on the list is to schedule a meeting with your child's teacher preferably within the first month of classes, as well as every after grading period or semester. Through this, you get to communicate with your child's teacher constantly and ask for updates and progress. This way you get to stay in the same page and regularly monitor your child's schooling.

Second on the list is to never forget to oversee your children's work and review all of their graded tests and activities. This is important because you get to see the current standing of your child in every subject he or she is taking. You get to monitor his or her strengths and weaknesses. And through this, you can improve further the strengths of your child and focus more with his or her weaknesses.

Do not forget to express appreciation to your child's teachers and educators several times during the school year. By this simple gesture, you send a message to them that as a parent, you are grateful for their hard-work, not just for your child but for all of their other students. After all, teaching is not an easy profession. It requires a ton of sacrifices for your students and it deserves recognition and appreciation.

One way of showing appreciation to your children's teacher is by physically helping out as much as you can in their school. You can consider volunteer opportunities such as organizing fund-raisers for projects in the school, joining parent-teacher conferences and actively participating in it, or by merely helping out in classroom meetings or field trips. This act of simple gestures will surely go along way and would benefit your relationship with your child's teacher.

Third on the list is to help your child in whatever endeavors he or she faces in school. Help your child set a time and place for homework and school assignments. This way, you can monitor your child's school works hands on which will greatly improve his or her performance. Help your kid to have a routine schedule in order to make studying second nature and more easy. Do not forget to provide moral support, materials and encouragement.

Fourth on the list is to energize your child's hope, especially if you see that they are struggling with school or a particular subject that they find really hard. A student who does not believe he can get through school will sooner or later give up and go to a downward spiral. These students need to believe that they can do and get through it. And who would better give them that encouragement and hope than their parents themselves. With a growing sense of achievement and motivation, your child will become more eager to learn new things and master their strengths.

Fifth on the list is to decrease TV and internet consumption for better focus and academic success. Since almost all young growing child today spend an average of three hours a day in multimedia, it distracts them from studying and school. Do not let them watch destructive shows because this will have permanent damage to their behaviors and attitudes. By decreasing this consumption, they will have more time to be productive in their studies and excel in school. And if they actually achieve this, you can reward them with extra hours of watching their favorite TV shows or surfing the internet.

The last thing on the list is to always love and understand your kid no matter what. As a parent, you would know that failure is inevitable in everyone's life. Your child may face a couple of failures along the way. The best thing to do about this is to always avoid critical reactions. Failing is hard enough for your child to accept. Do not make it worse by spur-of-the-moment commentaries. Express love to your child despite of his or her grades. However, do not forget to talk about it and adjust his or her studying habits in order for improvement to happen.

Good parenting involves focusing not just for your children's well-being, but for their education as well. This is a key factor in a growing child's life because this becomes an avenue for growth and learning. Information is such a powerful thing and can be gained through education. Your kids need this. Helping them get this will also help them achieve and be successful at something when they grow up too soon.

Chapter 17: Parenting Styles

In our positions as parents, counselors and role models to our children. We find out that naturally, we pick up parenting styles which affect the up bring of a child. Not only the up bring but the child's well-being, strength and over-all manner and conduct. A style which gives love and support with the perfect blend of discipline has been the best and reliable structure available. Children who are brought up using this style are always happy and confident. Furthermore, there are several factors which contributes to a child's behavior and functioning such as the parent's approach to discipline, communication, level of warmth and nurturing as well as the control level.

Basically, we have three parenting styles. However, Maccoby & Martin identified a fourth parenting style which has now become something rampart in this 21st Century. The idea behind you knowing your parenting style would help you in understanding what kind of parent you are and how you can work on yourself.

First we have the authoritarian parenting style. This is a style that majors on control. Parent have complete control. The Captain from the movie Sound of Music symbolizes a perfect example of an authoritative style of parenting. Under these parenting style you have strict rules and schedules. Parents are not parenting, they are RULERS controlling the house. Studies have been able to show that children being raised by authoritarian parents may appear well behaved. But this is only a façade. This parenting style produces children who are less resourceful and have low self-esteem.

Next is the permissive parenting style. This is a direct opposite of the authoritarian style. The parents of Jane belong to this category. They allow the child to take control. No rules, no regulations everything seem very lax. Even if rules are made, they are made to be broken. Parents using this style of parenting feel that their children should be free thinkers, they should be able to explore the world and learn for themselves. The failure of this style is that children don't really learn the rules. Since there are no active rules there is nothing to learn. There is no difference between right or wrong and punishment is seen as temporal pain. If a child is being raised by a permissive parent, he is typically irresponsible and would definitely have poor self-discipline.

While the parents are most likely to develop depression and anxiety.

Democratic parenting style follows. It is the blend of authoritarian and permissive parenting style. The democratic parent would set rules but would fail to enforce them. They are the ones that would collect a child's phone to be seized for one week and would end up giving him/her the phone on the second day. What the democratic parents are after is for the child to understand why the rules are in place. For a democratic parent, he/she would always want the child to understand what is wrong and why it is wrong. Children and parents work together, handle conflicts and reason problems in a respectable manner. Parents using this parenting style are talkers. They keep talking in order to keep everyone involved in the family.

The last parenting style we would talk about which is becoming popular day by day is the Neglectful/Uninvolved parenting. This style comprises of disengagement and emotional distance. Parents here show little warmth and responsiveness. Most homes where the father and Mother are business tycoons have this kind of parenting style activated. The child is neglected by the parents. The parents feel that once they can provide for the child, that's all. Children raised under this parenting style would no doubt function poorly in the society. 98% of Juvenile offenders are products of uninvolved parenting. What's worse is that children raised by these neglectful parents would most likely have poor cognition and struggle with social and emotional skills.

Now you know where you belong. What can you do? How can you work on yourself to become a better you? Success wouldn't come if we are not prepared for it. What we should have is a clear balance between the appropriate demands from a child and expectations. Warm emotional responsiveness gotten from reliable predictors which are mostly as a result of the child's emotion should be given to the child.

Chapter 18: Communicatingwith Toddlers

Eleven Principles of Effective Communication For Good Relationship

Communication serves as the basis for any kind of relationship, be it a marriage relationship, mother- father relationship, parent to child, child to another child etc. The roles of communication in any relationship cannot be overemphasized. Now, we are talking about toddlers her and even the roles of communication applies to them the most.

First, what is communication? The very definition of communication is the exchange of ideas from each side with adequate feedback. When the possibility of exchange of ideas is blocked, then the likelihood of reaching a mutual understanding is reduced. Effective communication includes sending the message you want to deliver, in a way it can be understood by the other party and receiving an immediate response. Communication is very important in families as it allow each member respect the wants and needs of each other. We definitely love our children and what them to grow up happy, healthy and responsible, then we really need to work on our communication skills. Why is effective communication important? It is, because our children also love us and want our guidance, support and approval. An effective communication modifies the way your child would communicate with others, from communication children learn values from our words, our postures and our tones. An effective communication skill with our children helps us to address problems or situations in a positive and healthy way. Having established this fact that communication serve as the base for a good relationship we need to know if good relationship or effective communication is really possible. Yes and yes, it is possible, below are some basic principles of good parent/child communication:

You can communicate without the interest of the other party. You need to let your child know that you are interested in him or her, you are involved and you are ready to help when needed.

Give your child all attention when he is communicating. Turn off the television, put the newspaper down, and raise your gaze from your mobile phone.

Make sure your conversations are private except if any other person is involved.

Embarrassment would only cause resentment and hostility. Don't embarrass them. You may be surprised that this applies to toddlers too.

You should get down to your child's level when you want to talk, don't tower over your child.

If you are angry, regain your temper before making an attempt to communicate.

Be an active listener and try to make an effort to be one even when you are tired. Genuine active listening is very difficult and hard work. We would talk more about this in this chapter.

Don't jump into conclusions when your children are opening up to you. Even if toddlers sometimes communicate incoherently most of the time, they are still saying something, they still want to tell you something. Be patient to listen to them.

Assist him or her to take the right steps when they come for advice.

Encourage the child's attempt to communicate, praise his or her effort. Children need a lot of encouragement and support at their tender age.

Don't use foul languages or words which put others down. Toddlers tend to imitate everything they see and hear. When I say everything, I mean everything.

This chapter would be very empty and incomplete without explaining the importance of words of encouragement and praise. As a parent, you should know that children thrive on positive attention and you are to give that to them. You can make use of some of the following phrases or all:

Yes Good Fine… .

Excellent!

That's right Correct

Wonderful! I like the way you do that…

I'm impressed

I am proud of you

That's good Wow!

Much better

You are really improving at. . .

You showed a lot of responsibility . . .

I appreciate the way you . . .

You are great at . . .

I am sure glad you are my son/daughter. . .

I LOVE YOU

You can also learn to show them how you fell by telling them the following:

Smile for me…

High five

A pat on your shoulder.

Scatter their hair gently with your fingers and smile.

You can tickle them, laugh with them, and give them a warm hug.

"If a child lives with criticism, he learns to condemn. If a child lives with hostility, he learns to fight. If a child lives with ridicule, he learns to be shy. If a child lives with fear, he learns to be shy. If a child lives with fear, he learns to be apprehensive. If a child lives with shame, he learns to feel guilty. If a child lives with encouragement he learns to be confident. If a child lives with acceptance, he learns to love. If a child lives with recognition, he learns it is good to have a goal. If a child lives with fairness, he learns justice. If a child lives with security, he learns to have faith in himself and those about him. If a child lives with friendliness, he learns the world is a nice place in which to live to love and be loved."-Anonymous

I wonder why a wonderful quote like the above should be anonymous, well it explains itself, what more can I say?

The other part of this chapter is going to talk more exclusively on listening in communication.

SLLR Method of Becoming An Active Listener

Just as we have explained that the importance of communication cannot be overemphasized in any relationship as well as toddler to parent relationship. It is fundamental for us to know how to listen in communication. It has been established that the mind of a toddler is adventurous, just like any other child. He wants to explore the world, understand more than you are letting him and do more than you can allow. They are always communicating to family, friends and even their toys. Remember we mentioned the imaginative aspect of their memory and how it helps growth, learning and behavioral make up. Their imaginative minds communicate with their toys, they turn a moving car into something quite different from what it is and other things around them. In the vocalization and socialization aspect of a toddler we see that when he/she is `15 months old, the ability to use 10-15 words is harnessed and fully utilized, the ability to say no, the ability to indicate when diaper is wet and also the ability to use phrase composed of adjectives and nouns becomes useful. These are all manners or forms of communication and our duty is to listen.

Picture this:

You are in a child care center, 19 month-old Gift is clinging to you, her and crying as they enter. You pull Gift's hands from your arm, saying, "Don't be such a crybaby and go play." You walk into the pediatrician's waiting room in another instance and Daniel climbs dangerously high on a furniture. He throws his toy at his mother when she calls his name. Instead of doing the needful, his mother laughs nervously and says quietly, "I don't know what to do with him." In another instance one year-old Melissa yanks on a locked kitchen cabinet while her father is cooking. He finds her and says, "Oh-I see you are trying to get into this cabinet, but these glass pans are for me only. Let's make a drawer with some plastic kitchen things for you. You can use them to while I cook."

The above scenarios show us that child-parent interactions is differ from each other. You can see that the interaction between Melissa and her father is harmonious and developmentally appropriate.

Young children including toddlers feel valued when parents listen to what they have to say. We all know that listening to kids is not always easy, but children think differently and sometimes they may not have the words to express themselves plainly. Listening is more than just hearing, it all about understanding the feelings embedded in the child's words and taking the positive action. In listening, for the soul aim of having a good relationship with your child, active listening should be employed.

What is active listening? Active listening is the best type of listening. Even in learning and other types of relationship. Here, it involves giving your child your undivided attention when he/she seeks you out for conversation. It's not just hearing, it requires using your intellect, feelings and even physical response to attract, attain and give information about your interaction. In active listening, you can use the following Stop-Look-Listen-Respond (SLLR) method:

Stop: You should stop whatever you are doing and pay attention to your child whenever they try communicating. Children love attention, and once you give that to them they open up, they need you to be focused on them.

Look: This is where we really need to know the importance of eye contact, facial expressions and body language. As a parent, you should look for nonverbal cues which may give you a hint on your child's thought and feelings.

Listen: Listen to what he/she is trying to say. Make up for the lapse in incoherent words and pay special attention to the tone of voice. Is he sounding angry? You should realize that they may be communicating in several messages and most may be unspoken.

Respond: make sure you use eye contact during the conversation and nods, "mmm-hmms". Smile, touch to confirm your attentiveness and make the necessary adjustment.

Seven Parenting Attributes to Build Great Relationship

Building a good relationship entails a lot, and one of it is making a relationship deposit. Imagine a deposit jar where you have coins labelled as praise, hugs, high fives, play, listen, etc. You have a good relationship with your child if you make these deposits. Even as a parent, it may not be easy to build a firm relationship with your child than building relationship with others. Having said that, you should make these deposits a regular thing in your relationship with your child, each day you should show all or at least some of the relationship building attributes. Here are the seven parenting attributes for building positive relationships with a child:

Spend quality time with your child. Both of you can work on a project together.

Acknowledge the child's effort in anything. Give encouragement for positive behaviors such as hugs, high fives, thumbs up after accomplishing task.

Make use of empathy, a relationship-building strategy that helps you interact and value what you have.

Play games with him or her and play outside.

Post your child's work on social media, your computer screen or hang them on you walls.

Ask them questions every time. With this you get an update on what they like and don't.

Make sure you adopt your child's ideas and stories. Especially when painting or participating in any activity, give them that freedom.

As you build positive relationship with your child, your potential influence the child's behavior and grows exponentially. This means that children cue in on the presence of meaningful and caring adults. They attend differentially and selectively and this gives me the impression that what you give is what you get. Listen to what they really want and give that to them. I must confess, communication is not easy, but it is necessary. Strengthening the relationship that exist between you and your child through active listening, influences the future of the child.

Chapter 19: Accidents Happen

Being a parent can be stressful. Especially as your little one gets more curious about the world around them. Children love to touch things, smell them, put them in their mouth, etc. They explore the world around them using their senses. Sometimes, this leads to accidents. Okay, a lot of times this leads to accidents. It can be frustrating, and you may feel like you are at your wits end. Just remember, it takes a few minutes to clean a mess; however, it takes years to mend a broken spirit.

This chapter is about accidents that are common with toddlers and how to handle these without destroying a child's desire to learn. These accidents will be delivered in a story style to make them enjoyable, and maybe you can laugh along with them so that when the time comes, you too can laugh at the simple things in life and give your child a whole lifetime of learning desire.

Don't Cry Over Spilled Milk

One of the most common parental frustrations is generally children spilling their beverages, or their food. Most parents buy the plates that suction cup to the table, and the no spill cups, so they do not have to clean up a ton of spills. This is not the case for the McGee family. They know that spills happen, and they decided that if their child wanted to spill something, she would find a way no matter what gadgets they bought.

As fate would have it, little Kaitlyn happened to do just that. It was not good timing either. Mrs. McGee was having a stressful day. It seemed that nothing was going right, and she felt like she was about to pull her hair out. The washer wouldn't drain, the sink was backed up, and she couldn't find her favorite pair of jeans.

Kaitlyn decided she would help her mom out by pouring herself some milk. She didn't want to bother her already upset mother by asking for help, so she went to the fridge and pulled out the gallon jug. At first, it seemed like things were going great! She got the cap off and got the gallon over to the kiddie table with no problem. However, her 2-year-old arms were not strong enough to tip the milk, and she dropped the open jug onto the floor.

Mrs. McGee heard the noise and went to see what was going on. She found Kaitlyn in the kitchen surrounded by their last gallon of milk, which covered the kitchen floor. Immediately, she became angry.

They could not get more milk until her husband got paid 2 days later, and now, they had no milk. As the words "How could you be so stupid?!" started to leave her mouth, Mrs. McGee looked into her child's eyes.

Kaitlyn looked so upset with herself; her mother found it impossible to be angry. Instead of asking the hurtful question she almost uttered, she changed her tune.

"Why didn't you ask for help?" She asked Kaitlyn softly.

"I wanted to help," Kaitlyn said.

"That is a wonderful thing to want to do, but sometimes, you still need assistance with. This is one of those things. Now, I will get us some towels, and we can clean this up together."

Mrs. McGee grabbed a couple of towels and showed her daughter how to clean up the mess she had made. She even showed her some fun ways, such as using your feet and doing a twist dance to sop up the milk. By the time they were done, they were both laughing and in good spirits, nearly forgetting that they were even cleaning up at all.

If the mother in this story had let her initial question of "How could you be so stupid?" slip off her tongue, she could have really hurt her daughter's self-esteem. A lot of parents will get angry, and angry words never heal open wounds. It is extremely important to remember, no matter how hard your day is, never let it get in the way of teaching your child a life lesson.

Children pick up on your emotions more than you may realize. So even something as simple as saying "It's fine. It happens." and cleaning up angrily can squelch your child's desire to try new things because they will be afraid to anger you. They also won't learn the value of cleaning up their own messes because they will feel like making a mess is a bad thing and cleaning up makes people angry.

Talk to your child; explain the mistake. However, do not belittle them. Use it as a time to teach them something new. You will be giving them a great foundation for the rest of their lives.

Don't Shatter Souls over Shattered Glass

It is no secret in life that toddlers can be rambunctious. They love to run, play, and jump. This is because they are learning all the cool things that their body can do. Unfortunately, they generally don't always have the best balance. This can lead to falls, scrapes, bruises, and broken furniture. Toddlers are also learning that if they do things wrong, they get in trouble. So, some of them may even tell little white lies because they feel that it will keep them out of trouble. The Tyler family went through this experience with their son Jaxon.

Jaxon recently turned three. Like most boys his age, he enjoyed pretending to be a superhero and going on adventures. Unfortunately for him, it was winter time, so most days, he had to stay inside. He felt cooped up because his mom wouldn't let him play superhero in their apartment. She said it was too dangerous. His dad agreed with his mom, so even when dad was in charge, Jaxon had to be calm. He couldn't stand it. So one day, when his dad was home while his mom was at work, Jaxon decided that he wanted to play superhero. He pretended to take and nap, and then, he waited until his dad also took a nap, and he began playing, trying to stay quiet.

Jaxon wanted to be superman, and to him, the couches and tables were the tall buildings he had to leap across to destroy the villain. For a while, things were going good. He was jumping from couch to couch without a problem. Suddenly, he had to jump to the coffee table to catch the villain before he escaped. Well, unfortunately for Jaxon, there was a vase of flowers in the way.

You guessed correctly. Jaxon knocked the vase off the table, and it crashed to the floor and shattered. The sound woke Jaxon's sleeping father immediately. Jaxon hurriedly jumped off the table and ran into his room before his father could see him as the culprit. Jaxon was worried that he would get in trouble for knocking the vase off, so he decided he would blame it on the villain he was chasing.

"Jaxon, can you come out here please?" His father asked calmly.

"Yes daddy?" Jaxon asked sweetly.

"Mind telling me how this vase got broken?"

"It was the villain, Dad. He knocked it off to get me in trouble." Jaxon said emphatically.

His father was very disappointed and considered sticking Jaxon immediately in time out. Instead, he decided on a different approach to curb the lying before it got out of hand. He decided to teach his son why lying was wrong.

"Jaxon. We are the only two here. I know who knocked the vase over. I will give you another opportunity to tell me the truth, and if you do not, you will get a time out." His father calmly explained.

"Okay. It was me. I was playing superhero even though I was supposed to be taking a nap." Jaxon said, looking at the floor.

His father picked him up and sat down, placing Jaxon on his lap.

"That is a lot better. You see, son. When you tell the truth, it is a lot better than lying. Sometimes you may get in trouble, but if you lie, you get in more trouble. Also, if you had continued to lie, I would not have been able to trust you anymore. You could tell me your name was Jaxon, and I may have a hard time believing it. Are you following?"

"I think so. Lying makes it harder to believe when someone tells the truth?" Jaxon replied.

"Exactly. You are a smart boy. I know it is hard living in a small apartment during the cold weather. Maybe after I get this glass cleaned up, we can move the furniture out of the way and play superhero together. However, for now, I want you to go to your room and sit for a bit and think about what I told you."

"Okay Dad."

Jaxon's father cleaned up the glass, and then, he and Jaxon played super hero throughout the house. They had a lot of fun.

Mr. Tyler could have just outright grounded his son for lying. However, he didn't want his son to think that either way he would get in the same amount of trouble. He wanted to make sure that his son knew the consequences of lying. By giving him another chance to tell the truth, he was teaching his son the value of being honest.

He also took the time to explain why lying was bad. It seems like a lot of parents are in the mentality that children should do what they are told with no explanation. Too many times, you hear a parent say "because I said so," when asked a question by their child. This mentality is very detrimental to child rearing because children feel as if their questions are not important. It also makes them more likely to rebel because they feel that there is no real reason for the rules. Taking the time to explain things to your child helps them to better understand why you say and do the things that you do.

Encourage your children to ask questions. It helps them gain understanding and can help your children better respect you, when they feel respected as well. Your children will grow, and it will help their minds develop.

Don't Degrade Your Big Kid, for a Potty Mistake

No one likes to be out in public and deal with their toddler going to the bathroom in their pants. However, sometimes it happens. Toddlers are so enthralled by the world around them that sometimes they do not pay attention to what is going on inside them. Sometimes, they miss out on the cues that tell them they need to go to the bathroom, so they end up having an accident in their pants.

The Kirtley family had this experience at a fair nonetheless. Their daughter Jada was 3 years old and had not had an accident since she was 2 years old. She was always diligent about letting her parents know when she had to go to the bathroom, so when she had an accident, they were not prepared. This story is about a family who handled the situation poorly and contains information on a better way to handle these situations.

Conclusion

Thank you again for downloading this book!

Yes, the journey is difficult. Nevertheless, if you follow the simple tips and aids that we have suggested, it will be extremely easy for you to perform the job singlehandedly. We hope that we have helped you discover the joys of being a mother along with sufficiently safeguarding you against all the potential pit holes of a planned or an unplanned single motherhood.

The first thing you need to remember about being a single mother is you need to make peace with your situation (this applies to unplanned single mothers). You play the most important role in your child's life; you need to make sure that you play it to perfection.

As long as you put your mind to it, you will realize that nothing is impossible.

The basic thing your kids need from you is love and attention. If you give them that, there is no reason for them to feel the need for the 'other' parent. Of course, there will be questions, and we hope you are now equipped to handle them in an efficient manner, after reading this book.

It may not be a smooth ride but learn to take it in your stride. Be ready to face the challenges that come along. Once you make yourself equipped to face these challenges, single motherhood becomes a much easier role than it is made out to be. Remember to have fun along the way and it will be a breeze.

After all, single or not, you are still a mother by instinct, so the job does come naturally to you. You just need to walk the extra mile to make up for the role of the other parent in your kids life and you will realize that the journey is much easier than it is made out to be.

We, thank you for taking the time out to read this book and sincerely hope that you become the mother you always wanted to be and provide your kids with all the love, care, attention and affection they need and deserve.

Thank you and good luck!